COME BACK TO LIFE

STOP
the EMPTINESS
and START
the JOURNEY
to
FEEL
the
HAPPINESS
INSIDE & OUT

MARKI SPACILOVA

COME BACK TO LIFE

STOP THE EMPTINESS AND START THE JOURNEY TO FEEL THE HAPPINESS INSIDE & OUT

MARKI SPACILOVA

Written by: Marki Spacilova
Edited by: Erik Seversen
Proofread by: Jessie Raymond
Second proofreading by: Jessica Schmidt
Formatted and layout by: Abdul Rehman

Title: Come Back to Life
Subtitle: Stop the Emptiness and Start the Journey to Feel the Happiness Inside & Out
ISBN: eBook 978-1-8383286-1-0
ISBN: Paperback 978-1-8383286-4-1

Category: Self-help book/eBook /Mind-Body-Spirit/ Spirituality/
Co-Marketing/Consultant-Lifestyle/Productivity

Self-Published Author: Marki Spacilova

Registered business address: 86-90 Paul Street, London, EC2A 4NE

Contact: connectwithmarki@authormarki.co.uk
Self-published author, Marki Spacilova reserves the right to terminate the link
to email address and the website at any time from the date of this book publication.

Photo of Marki Spacilova provided: © Sarka Pastrnakova Pesat

Cover design of the book: © Blackcardbooks

LIMITS OF LIABILITY/DISCLAIMER OF WARRANTY

Marki Spacilova is the self-published Author of this book. Please use this book wisely. If you have any medical conditions or health concerns, consult with your doctor first. I do not offer legal advice. This book contains content on legal criteria required to open your own business, however, it is recommended that you speak to an appropriate trained professional. This book is written according to the author's experience, testing, research, interviews and opinions including health and fitness topics. Therefore it is recommended that the reader consult with a nutritionist, fitness trainer, Kundalini yoga practitioner and all other trained professionals alluded to.

The information provided by the Author, both in this book and website, coaching service is intended to be used for educational, informational and support purposes only and does not constitute any medical or legal advice. If you read this book and follow any instructions contained therein without consulting an appropriate registered trained professional, you are doing so at your own risk.

You as the reader are required to take responsibility for your thinking and your actions based on your own reasoning and choices. The exercises may have helped the author, but they may not help you without the appropriate trained professional or expert opinion being referred to also. The author does not make any promise or guarantee that this publication will help you without using it in conjunction with your professional medical, legal representative or life coach.

The author does not intend to cause any type of harm related to the readers' use of information contained in the book. Every individual possesses unique needs and person-centred requirements, therefore, choose your appropriate medical, legal or business professional expert with as much appropriate due diligence as possible.

You are responsible and accountable for your own decisions, actions, and conduct in your life. Everything composed in this book has been carefully checked, considered, verified and therefore the content has been compiled and contains experiences, sources, and opinions believed to be accurate, however the author assumes no responsibility for any errors, omissions or mistakes in the content. Some aspects of author's experiences have been altered to protect the author Marki Spacilova and other people referred to in the publication.

This publication is intended to be a marketing tool to promote righteous compassion in our workplaces and unity, humanity and social justice for both employees, voluntary workers and captain's of industry.

Recommendation: Please, do not accept this book as a substitute or replacement for medical treatment, financial, legal, health, personal or trained professional guidance.

ABOUT THE AUTHOR

Marki Spacilova is an Author, Transformational Speaker, and Spiritual and Business & Productivity Coach. She didn't know why, but she felt she had to come to England. She left the Czech Republic in 2002. However, once moving there, where she once had a voice, she no longer had it. This fact sent her on a downward spiral. She began her journey of discovery not only to lead a fulfilling life, but also to find her true calling. That is helping others to revive themselves. Helping others to get back into their lives is the result of her own experience of feeling lost in life and not knowing what she wanted to do.

Marki's new book, "Come Back to Life: Stop the Emptiness and Start the Journey to Feel the Happiness Inside & Out," is written for those who feel that they are not good enough, feel stuck in life, or do not know their purpose in life. Some people think of creating their own eco-friendly business, but they are afraid to take on that responsibility.

In the past, Marki's corporate experience had been limited to lecturing people on what to do, more in a "Bossy" manner than being of service. This bossy manner was until she discovered the possibility of becoming a coach. Because of this journey, she developed her own unique system to help people regain control of their lives. From mastering the knowledge of the past, present, and future of time and action, she has encouraged many people to empower themselves and move forward in the direction of a life they truly want to lead.

Moreover, Marki coaches men and women on personal growth subjects, such as self-discovery and creating awareness. Equipped with years of intensive breakthroughs and study in understanding life and how to bring yourself to be in the present moment. She provides one-on-one and group coaching. She helps people listen to their inner voice, clear their mental fog, and discover their purpose with passion. Some transcend to become business leaders.

Marki's experience as a care professional for the elderly and an activity coordinator has given her deep insights into understanding and engaging with people. Her experience has led her to create workshops. Those workshops are about building a community that is interesting and engaging.

Besides, Marki has taken all of her good and bad experiences in business and her life into achieving one goal. Her goal is to bring her vision to help people discover their passion, utilise their talents, and bring their creativity to create a platform, so they can start to develop their projects. Her mission is to support inventive men and women by helping them to discover a deeper meaning in their experiences, talents, and purpose on Planet Earth.

No matter who you are or what background you come from, we can unite and have the same aim. We want to make a difference and be part of the community to help people and the planet Earth. You are welcome to join in.

Are you committed to that purpose?

"If you choose to combine the goals of helping like-minded people and creating an eco-friendly and sustainable business, you will become a united, transcended business leader yourself."

—Marki Spacilova

<u>Please, read the book to find out what it means.</u>

IN MEMORIAM OF MY FATHER

This book is written in memoriam of my father, Petr Spacil (1956 - 2019). My father was my idol; he was also exemplary. One of the most important lessons I learned from him was to be non-judgemental. He had a nickname, "Maticka" (meaning *Saint Mother* in English). While he was alive, he was a great father and a great son. He developed skills, just like his father, and he enjoyed creating DIY projects.

I would also like to dedicate this book to: Ludmila Zenaida Amalia Pond, also known as Mila Pond (1926 - 2021). She taught me how powerful it is to have an accountable listener. She was not exactly a counsellor or an accountability partner, however, whenever I needed to speak out loud to listen to myself, she was there to help me with that. I was going through an emotional transition without a spiritual life coach or any coach to lead me out of my emotional despair, but she helped just by listening. Any time I felt that way. I talked about it, and she had no answer. But I did. I'm eternally grateful for all she taught me.

ACKNOWLEDGEMENT

There are certain people, including friends, family, and colleagues who helped me and supported me throughout the process since I started to learn how to make a difference and began to write this book. Those people helped me with some advice, guidance or whatever I needed to progress step by step. Each individual contributed their assistance when I needed them most. Some of the people I would like to sincerely thank are: Roman A. Masaryk, Chuck Cibulka, Aleksander Korzynski, Weston Davis, Marcel Rebsamen, Pablo F. Rosero, Mirza Sheraz Altaf, Vincent Cheng, Patrick J. Mc Neill, blackcardbooks team and others who also taught me great lessons I can use for the rest of my life.

TABLE OF CONTENTS

CHAPTER ONE: Turning Negative Experiences into Positive Lessons.......2

CHAPTER TWO: Discovering What Prevents You from Taking Action. 10

CHAPTER THREE: Creating Change in Your Life 17

CHAPTER FOUR: Motivation from Within 23

CHAPTER FIVE: Your Unique Self-Care.. 29

CHAPTER SIX: Reconnecting Emotions and Feelings 36

CHAPTER SEVEN: Connecting Senses to Your Awareness 44

CHAPTER EIGHT: Tuning into Forgiveness and Making Amends 51

CHAPTER NINE: Creating a Pleasant Environment in Your Workplace, No Matter What.. 59

CHAPTER TEN: Becoming a United Transcended Business Leader 64

COMPANION EXERCISE BOOK.. 72

WHAT CAN YOU DO TO START? 95

ACKNOWLEDGEMENT OF CREDIBILITY IN THEIR EXPERTISE 96

COME BACK TO LIFE. WHY? BECAUSE WE ARE ALL EQUAL!

CHAPTER ONE

TURNING NEGATIVE EXPERIENCES
INTO POSITIVE LESSONS

We can take control of our life and our future. Now, what does life mean to you? For me, life is a journey from one situation to another. We can take advantage of this understanding by turning negative situations into positive life lessons. Life can be a journey toward our personal growth; a journey where we can move from pain to positivity. Hence, we have to be deliberately conscious enough to accept negativity and positivity as equally important parts of our journey through life. When we do this, transformation occurs in our lives; this transformation is not only good for ourselves but can also be inspiring to others.

In the past, I made many wrong choices because I did not know any better; choices that put me in bad situations, which caused me trouble in my life. I would make decisions from a negative outlook on life rather than an outlook of hope. After much introspection, I made the decision to make improvements and now, I can say I have grown stronger and wiser.

History—What I Know

Thanks to history, we have been able to understand the concept and principles of diverse cultures, ethics, and religions. We have all gone through similar learning processes; we've learnt about life, nature, and mysteries, and have also learnt about people and their stories. We've listened to popular theorists and have also read books and articles on experiments and discoveries.

However, it's not enough to know these concepts, principles, people, and inventions. The more important question is, with what we know, what are we creating for ourselves now?

The Present Moment and What We Have in Common

Some of us spend hours - even days - playing video games or scrolling through endless social media feeds. We do this because of the pressing need to escape from the present world. Most of the time, we procrastinate, neglecting what our own inner child needs as a result, just to live in the moment. We tell ourselves we want to do something different, something more productive and then we change our minds — on repeat.

When we plan to complete tasks, we often include the word, tomorrow. Tomorrow becomes another tomorrow, and as time goes on, we become uninterested. At the end of the day, we fail to get things done, because somehow, we have already forgotten what we wanted to do in the first place. Other times, we pile up our tasks. And the truth is, the more tasks we pile up, the less we want to deal with them; then we wonder why we're left with so much to do.

Our current way of life is no way to live. I mean, dreaming about the future is a great source of motivation, but to succeed, we need to back these dreams up with actions; these actions include changing our mindset and adding discipline.

The Idealistic Future

Imagining an idealistic future is great. But then, what most of us do, is to actually create unrealistic pictures of the future. We have big ideas, while the actions are small in comparison. This behaviour can stem from our experiences during childhood. This is why I often recommend introspection; it gives us a sense of history, causing a strong desire to change the present, and shape the future into what we think we want it to look like. However, most times, we choose to follow in the footsteps of our fathers and mothers rather than learn from our past experiences, since it is the easy way out.

There are those who learn from their past; for instance, some children might develop a passion for science because of health issues in the family. More specifically, the daughter of a cancer victim might devote her life to pursuing research towards a cure for cancer. In this case, we can say that pain and hardship has caused a positive reaction. This positive reaction might be used to prevent others from suffering from the same disease in the future. In this example, the tragic loss of one person's life through cancer has inspired entirely new research that would save the lives of many. Thus, a negative past can create a positive future.

Learning from the past is not limited to tragic circumstances. We can learn from mistakes as well.

For example, there was a time when I would play video games on my days off. I justified this by saying that I had no time to do anything else. In my job, I was a workaholic, so I convinced myself that playing video games was for my leisure, when in fact, it was my way of escaping from reality. It got to a point where I was escaping too much. When I learnt that I could change my mindset from negativity to positivity, I slowly and gradually replaced my addiction to games with self-care tasks and studies.

Studying and learning - about nature in particular - became a positive force in my life. The effect of doing new stuff that was productive made me feel a lot better. It is remarkable what a person can accomplish when passion and talents are explored, especially after we make the effort to learn from our mistakes like I did. The first thing you need to do is to identify if there are ways you could be more prudent with your time.

The Mindset of Transition

If you're like most people, you have conversations in your mind. While in certain cultures, it is called monkey mind, I like to call it self-talk or auto-suggestion.

For example, I used to say to myself, I am not good at technology. I cannot do it. I am not good enough. Sound familiar?

Well, having experienced negative self-talk first-hand, I can say for a fact that it is not easy to change it, but when you finally do, it is worth it. You have to remember this — words and beliefs are powerful spiritual tools that can be used for creation or destruction. Transformation entails a change in the mindset, and that comes with a price to pay — changing the negative self-talk. Once again, it is not easy, but I have a fun method that's easy to remember.

The cost of change:

(Framework Signature M.E.E.T A.L.I.)

● **Money** ● **Energy** ● **Effort** ● **Time** ● **And** ● **Life** ● **Itself**

Every journey requires a destination. The mind will always struggle to stay on track if we do not have a desired destination or target, we are aiming toward.

Without a clear direction:

- Something may go wrong.

- An outside force may prevent you from reaching your goal.

- You may be confused about what is acceptable, and that may be limiting.

- Your progress may be hindered.

In as much as we might want to be careful to avoid accepting negative self-talk within ourselves, we certainly need to avoid allowing negative words from others to affect our mindset too.

Let Go of Negativity

There are many forms of negativity, but the most dangerous one is when we lie to ourselves. We lie to ourselves when we choose to ignore the importance of personal growth and resort to complaining without creating a plan to change.

For example, let's assume someone from a different country did something to you or to someone you know. After this experience, it is possible that we create a sort of stereotype about this offence. We might even begin to think that everyone from that country is the same — if we believe that we cannot trust that person from one country, we also believe that we cannot trust anyone from that country.

This is simply wrong. It is a common misconception. This type of untruth can also turn into racism if it goes unchecked. No matter how much negativity exists within a person, everything can be healed and restored. The negative action of one person is an action from an individual, and not the entire group or race to which they belong.

It is important not to dwell on negatives. Instead, we should focus on the positive, since no negative action is permanent.

What can we do to change that pattern of fixed, negative thinking?

- Changing the mindset and perspective.
- Education.
- Journalling.
- Identifying and taking action steps toward changing negative thinking.

The next time a person offends you in any way, try to remember:

- First, an individual's mistake does not automatically represent others like them.
- Second, no negative situation is permanent.
- Third, there is always a place for growth to occur.

Transmuting Negative Thoughts into Positive Thinking

Positivity is an acceptance that every life matters no matter who they are, where they come from, what they have done, what they think about or what happened in the past. The future has the potential to be positive. Therefore, if we think positively in every aspect of our life, a positive future would be possible, and we will be a part of it.

What was in the past still exists in the present. However, what was in the past is not in the future — at least, not yet. Our decisions affect our future. Therefore, it is up to us to choose the best future possible by thinking positive thoughts as we move from past to present, and present to future.

The Principle of Past, Present and Future

This book is based on the principle of past, present and future. You can use this book at any stage of your life, whether you are faced with mild negativity, in a bad mood, or if you've just had an argument with a friend. It is imperative to understand the principle of past, present, and future.

Why? Because in knowing the reasons for our experiences, we know our purpose for our future. This means you can create a specific person-centred strategy, suitable for you to reach the goal, the idea, the mission, the purpose and the need you want to fulfil.

The principle of the past, present and future gives you an insight to where you have been, and what has led to what you are doing right now. You may think about the past, and you may want to bring back your memories, because you feel those memories somehow help you to grow; however, holding on to the past will not help you to move forward.

When we do not know any better, we create environments that are comfortable for us. We tend to repeat the past experiences because we seem to prefer a painful past that is familiar, instead of moving forward in our present — to an unknown territory. We do this frequently without knowing the consequence of our actions/thoughts. We hardly pay attention to the fact that we can learn from that experience.

How can we use our past as a life lesson?
That is the true principle of the past.
"Breathe and Live!"

CHAPTER TWO

DISCOVERING WHAT PREVENTS YOU FROM TAKING ACTION

"Decide what you want to be remembered for.
What skills, talents and passions can you contribute to help
like-minded people and our planet Earth? You have a say in what
you plan to do with your life, and your choices do affect only you.
Make a difference. Take control over your life and be confident
in your future…" "Be and stay positive."

- Marki Spacilova

Opportunity to Change

We all are capable of change, but the hard part is, change without action is impossible. Many of us grew up surrounded by negativity from every angle of our lives. What happened while we were growing up shaped our different perspective on life. Growing up, we learnt how to think and cope with struggles and difficulties. However, as mentioned in the first chapter, we can choose how we want to react to situations in our life. Do we want to be part of the problem or part of the solution?

Too often, situations in life seem to be more negative than positive. However, I have found that each time I have a problem, a struggle or some difficulty, there is something for me to learn. The important part is finding the right answer — the point that can be learned. However, this varies from person to person. Also, there is the fact that what is easy for you might not be easy for someone else.

The same is true about finding the answer to a negative situation, problem, or struggle. Seeing the lesson that needs to be learned might be difficult, depending on the individual. Practice can make a person better at answering questions. It is possible to become better at recognizing the lessons to be learned from negative moments in life, so that it can be easier to change negativity into positivity.

Fighting Ego with Intuition and logic

The self talk weighs the pros and cons of ego vs intuition vs logic That can be a very interesting conversation in our head, which can influence our quality of life.

Ego – You might tell yourself that you are not good enough. It is the job of the ego to protect you from failure. It is automatic. If you, as a person, don't remain strong, then your ego will keep telling you to stay in your comfort zone, which, in my opinion, is a place of stagnation.

Intuition – Your intuition might say there is an opportunity to take, despite that there might be some risks. It might say, just do it.

Logic – Your logical mindset might tell you to stay calm. It can take control and say, "let's try it, and we will see."

We have ego telling us to stay in our comfort zone; we have intuition saying to take risks; and we have logic going back and forth… it would be madness to have a conversation-loop like this without resolution. Therefore, it is important to be conscious of the ego, intuition, and logic, so we can rationally decide which one can best move us closer to our goals.

Don't miss this tip!

Take control of your life by choosing to take responsibility for what you think and how you act because that determines your future and who you are. Break your invisible chains and motivate yourself to get out of that rut and dormant way of life.

Fear

Fear is another factor that can determine how good we feel about our lives. It does not have to stop you from being the CEO of your life, or from being a transcended business leader. We will define this concept later in the final chapter.

When you think of fear, you have a gut feeling; that means you're intuitive, but your instinct will want to protect you. You may be too paranoid to go ahead with something that scares you, but then, when you learn what you are truly afraid of, you're able to try to be a better version of yourself.

There might be parts of your life where experiences and lessons are infrequent, meanwhile, you need those experiences to have more clarity. This requires you to adapt quickly to circumstances; to act fast and make decisions immediately regarding any circumstances you are in. If you think and act on the subject with clarity, you can continue to progress toward a good outcome. You quickly recognise clarity and upgrade your skills as well in that moment. That means you just learnt another required skill needed for your personal growth. You just upgraded yourself to be a better you. Is fear holding you back from progressing step-by-step to become a better you?

"Fear is nothing more than an indication that there is something to learn; find out what it is and learn it."

—Marki Spacilova

This book is written for anyone who wants to improve their life, but it is specifically aimed at professional men and women who feel stuck and tired of conflict, who are stressed, and want to break free from their invisible chains.

I think it is important not to forget about things like nature. In entrepreneurship, important things like this are often neglected. Nature must be always in the back of our minds. Our jobs can have an impact on nature and the world around us.

Being a conscious tradesperson is a great way to help the planet. Being an environmentally friendly construction contractor, an ecologically conscious scientist, or a socially aware professional business owner are all ways we can each contribute to improving ourselves, but also to making the world a better place. When do you want to master your life and become the CEO of your life?

No matter who you are or what background you come from, we can unite and have the same aim. We all want to make a difference and be part of the community to help people and the planet Earth. You are welcome to join in. Do you share that purpose?

> *"If you choose to combine helping like-minded people and*
> *creating an eco-friendly and sustainable business, you will become*
> *a united transcended business leader yourself."*
>
> —Marki Spacilova

Money: Patterns of Earning and Spending

This is the magic of money. That's what I call it. We go to work and back home almost every day. The point is, we bring our earnings home but then we spend it quickly. We need to go shopping because we have run out of groceries and supplies are missing in the bathroom. When you go to the shop, and you see the high prices, you hand over your hard-earned money for very little. Many live from pay-check to pay-check, and no matter how much we try, we cannot save enough money to have the life we want. Whenever I think about money, I feel there is not enough for me. Is that so? Why would I think that? Money does not grow on trees. Really? I thought it did.

Let's try to imagine that money does grow on trees. There does exist a plant called a money tree, officially named **Pachira Aquatica**. If that plant could have coins in spendable currency and produce more each time the leaves drop, imagine how much money we would have?

That would be a dream come true, wouldn't it? But that is a fantasy, and we need to come back to reality. Think of why we cannot keep the actual money we have. Do we always have to spend it? Money has become a huge factor in our world. Throughout history, money has existed and probably will continue to exist, whether it is physical or digital. The question is, how should we live with money?

Generally, humans do not want ups and downs, especially the downs. How can we solve the constant problem of unexpected expenses popping up at the wrong time? You name it. When does a car need to be fixed? Or a water heater needs to be replaced? Life happens all the time, and we cannot control it. Or can we?

We can budget and buy things we can afford. This is a smart way to live. With a bit of planning and some effort, we should be able to save 10% from every pay check. If you set this rule for yourself and continue to follow it, that 10% cannot be used until you have savings equivalent to six months of your salary. Once you have built up the six-month milestone savings amount, you can think about buying simple things to make your life more pleasant. An even better option would be to invest the money, so it will continue to grow. Hence, it is recommended to speak to a registered professional financial advisor to ensure you are doing the right thing.

With good spending habits and a solid amount of money saved, saving for retirement becomes less of an issue, and your future will be more secure. But then again if you love what you do, there is no need to retire anyway.

Not Knowing Is Like a Punishment

Ignorance feels horrible and can prevent us from acting; humans generally dislike uncertainty, just like they do not like punishment. I remember a time when I was overthinking a situation about my future. I could not see what I would be doing in five years. I couldn't even see what I would be doing in less than a year from that time. How then could I be expected to know what I was going to do in 20 years? I was spending a lot of time educating myself, but I did not know if what I was learning and studying would help me in my future.

Then I realised two things:
1. I realised that I loved what I was studying.
2. I also realised the information came very easily for me.

These two revelations made me certain that I was on the right track.

One thing that stuck out to me about the learning process was, I had to have a true eagerness to learn the subject for it to make the most impact for me. When I am enthusiastic about learning, I find the subject easier for me to learn. That means it is the right fit for me. But when I was questioning my energy spent on learning, I had to work on learning to trust myself and overcome my doubts. Back then, I was going back and forth about the thoughts in my head, until I weighed my options, and ultimately, I realised that my choice to pay the price of time and energy for my studies was going to help me move closer to the life I wanted to live.

When we decide to take control and truly live the life we choose, suddenly, everything falls into place. Opportunities become more visible. We find ways to be motivated. With direction in our lives, we can gracefully create a fulfilling life for ourselves.

CHAPTER THREE

CREATING CHANGE IN YOUR LIFE

"When you know your calling, only you will know what you should study."

—Marki Spacilova

As you read this chapter, think about these questions:

- How do you feel about learning new knowledge and gaining wisdom?

- What stories do you tell yourself?

Stories to Tell

While some people have close relationships with family and friends, many other people experience distance from relatives. Why is this? What keeps some people away from close relationships with family and friends? Simply, I would say that many do not feel the need to keep in touch with friends and family because they have nothing new to share or say.

When something new happens to us, we like to share stories with others. We like to tell others our news, but what if our lives become so routine, there are no new stories to tell? What if we do not have any active adventures, and there is nothing new to share?

When someone asks you, "What's new?" what do you say?

A very common response to this question is, "Nothing."

Quite often, people get into fixed routines without new events, and without new challenges. Everything is the same, day after day. The conversation that starts with, "What's new?" ends quickly because there really isn't much to say. This is exactly what happens when we keep ourselves in our comfort zone, since there is no new story to tell.

The day might sound like this: We go to work. We come back home. Somewhere along the line, there might be children to feed and play with or teach about life. And then life flows rather quickly, and we feel like we're not accomplishing anything.

Choose to connect with people. Be one of the people who always has something to say; someone who always seeks out new experiences in life that provide learning and enrichment.

Self-Isolation

Not only do many people avoid sharing stories with their family and friends, but they also tend to self-isolate. Sometimes, this may occur because of conscious choice, but most times, it happens subconsciously, without us giving it much thought. The most important thing to note here, however, is that self-isolation can be a very dangerous, and possibly unhealthy place to be. Self-isolation can come as a result of negative conversations with others.

Negative conversations and constant complaints create the opposite effect of optimistic conversations. Negative talk and constant complaints can be draining for the listener. After a while, these listeners will become less interested in calling you or seeing you, and then you're at risk of spending more time alone.

Typical questions you may ask yourself:

- Why is this happening to me?
- Why is it always me who is alone?
- What have I done?

At certain points in time, life can be a routine state of existence. When we start to ask, "Why me?" we are not in control of our own life. It means you've become a victim of life.

- Do you want to stay in the same comfort zone and do nothing? No.
- Do you want to get out of your comfort zone? Yes.

Then choose to engage with life rather than just letting life pass you by.

Information Fatigue

There is so much to learn in life. We could go crazy, trying to learn everything. It is like choosing the perfect massage. Do you know how many types of massages there are? Swedish, Thai, Japanese, Shiatsu, deep tissue... The list goes on and on. Then you must factor in the variations of each type, and the individual styles from the various massage therapists. One could live an entire lifetime, trying to find the perfect massage for themselves.

The same is true about information you learn and absorb. But should we give up? Not wanting to learn is a sign of information fatigue or avoidance of personal growth. Either way, that can be a common problem for people who are trying to greatly improve themselves. How can we avoid this problem? There are many options to choose from when it comes to learning. Once you agree to learn new things, it is a good idea to have a plan and follow it.

However, many people who want to change their life try to take on too many lessons at once. Be aware of shiny object syndrome, as you may get overwhelmed. There is also a tendency of starting to procrastinate. It starts by taking a small break; the small break becomes longer, and our thoughts wander until we find a good excuse as to why we should not continue with our lesson. Our overzealous plan to try to learn too much at once becomes a hindrance to our progress rather than an asset to our progress.

"You can fulfil your purpose using your passion based on your talents."

—Marki Spacilova

Honesty with Yourself and Others

While I already mentioned how great it is to tell stories, the worst thing we can do is make up stories to make our lives seem better. If there is nothing new to tell others because we refuse to practise a new way of living, then make it a challenge for yourself to discover a new interest or explore a passion you've had for a while. It is important to avoid lying to ourselves and others by creating stories about things that we have not done — even if these are things we intend to do.

In order for us to get going on our goals and actually create real stories, the WHY has to be as strong as Hercules. When this happens, what you want becomes so strong that the universe will deliver it to you on a golden platter. The things you most strongly desire will manifest in your life.

Each unique individual has their unique perspective and opinions. Let them give you advice. Input and suggestions from others can greatly improve your personal and professional growth. It can help you grow your confidence and self-esteem. It is also important that the ideas of others are aligned with you and your goals.

If you are not sure that another person's ideas match your unique character, then question that. Ask them for an explanation based on the past, present and future. That will provide you with an evaluation to help with the evolution of your personal growth and change of direction. Working with others is a great way to see if you need to change your current strategy, or if a transition is part of the evolution in your life.

Start with a Small Decision

At some point, everyone is going to recognise that a change needs to be made in their life. This happened to me too.

I became aware of what I was doing. I knew I was addicted to watching TV, playing video games, and chatting on social media. At one point, I even slept until midday because of my shift into these habits. I stayed awake too late at night doing these things as I chose to escape from my reality.

Fun Fact: I found out that nobody can motivate you to do anything you do not want to do yourself.

Once I firmly decided I wanted to change, I began reducing the time I spent on TV and gaming, and instead, chose to attend masterclasses that could help me stay on track. While deep-level motivation must start from within yourself, joining a group of others to support you is the best way to achieve sustainable results.

Attending scheduled masterclasses is a very powerful way to create positive changes in your life. Masterclasses are often only 30 to 90 minutes, and they can have a very strong positive impact in helping you create the changes you want in your life and to help you reach your goals. With the core of self-motivation and the support and accountability from a masterclass, you can achieve anything.

CHAPTER FOUR

MOTIVATION FROM WITHIN

"How can you get yourself motivated to accomplish change in your life?
There might be many answers to this, but ultimately, motivation
comes from within us. However, massive, and rapid growth comes
from the help of a mentor or coach — someone who is few steps
ahead of you and has taken the journey before you."

– Anonymous

Big Goals

While goals are incredibly important, we need to be wary of creating unrealistic dreams in combination with fear. When dreams become frightening, we can limit ourselves. When fear surfaces, our brains unconsciously try to protect us from fear. We tend to avoid acting. In this case, we dream about the future, yet we do nothing to achieve our future dream.

Similarly, if you have a big goal without a plan, then you cannot hope to achieve it, it will never happen. Goals cannot be fulfilled without action. Making a bucket list and talking about it is not enough without a plan. Maybe your goal is to have a big boat, big house, and healthy family by next year, but you don't know where to start.

Setting goals without making a plan is a good way to go nowhere. Without a plan to guide you toward the goal, something will always get in the way.

Common causes of postponed goals:

- Life happens.
- Your water heater stops running.
- Car breaks down.
- Concerns about job security.

Each of these things might act as a hindrance to achieving your goals if you haven't prepared for them in advance. Having a plan can help minimize obstacles.

Big Plans

There are several types of circumstances that cause us to give up on our dreams or goals. Having a big plan with a short time line to achieve it is another way to stop us from reaching goals. While having a plan is necessary, giving ourselves an unrealistic deadline can create frustration and keep us from reaching the goal.

Many people say to think big, start following your dream, and set a deadline for your goals. Yes, I agree with this. However, it is impossible to achieve a plan within an unrealistic timeline. In order to avoid this pressure, we need to think of a reasonable timeframe to achieve the goal we set.

Let's use exercise for an example. When you are new to weight lifting, it wouldn't be wise try to lift ten kilograms if your muscles are used to lifting two kilograms. Your results would likely be: stress, fatigue, and failure. The same is true when you are working toward any goals. Set a goal, break it down into milestones, set a realistic time line and continue making steps toward achieving it.

When life gets in the way, and we become frustrated by not meeting unrealistic deadlines for goals, we postpone our goal or we give up, which is the worst thing you can do. Giving up on your goals is the first step in giving up on what you want for your life. Life is precious, so, be realistic about your dreams and don't give up.

Doing Nothing

The worst thing you can do when you have a big goal, and a realistic timeline is to do nothing. We cannot just think about the big plan, we must act on it! The action steps should be in place, since we know that we cannot teleport from A to B. We cannot say, "I want to buy a house today," when we do not have the money in place. But just because we don't have everything in place right now doesn't mean we shouldn't have the goal and have the plan.

That's the reason why the plan is important: when we think of a goal in our mind, the universe tries to help us accomplish that need. This is the secret of the law of attraction.

Procrastination

There are several reasons why we procrastinate. It has something to do with the complexity of our brain. When we try to absorb information too quickly, we do not let the brain process the information, and then we lose interest in continuing our learning.

Procrastination starts to occur without us consciously thinking about it, just like our subconscious mind is still active as we sleep. We need both the right quantity of sleep and the right quality of sleep. Likewise, the brain requires more than quality learning; it requires learning in the right quantity as well.

It is vital to have rest days to process new information. When you take time to think about what you've learned, you find little details you might have missed, and that is often when you have your "aha" moments.

Every "aha" moment means the brain has processed and internalised the new information. If you find yourself procrastinating often, it is because you're not giving yourself the time to process new information, and your brain is unconsciously trying to avoid new things.

Motivation and Smiling

Do you ever lie with your face? What I mean is, do you ever smile on the outside while you are feeling sad on the inside? Well, this might be good for you. When we smile, we take one step toward feeling good on the inside. We can create positivity with our smile alone and then begin to feel that positivity on the inside too.

We may not always feel happy, and we might not want people to know how we truly feel, so we put on a smile. That actually works in our favour. If we smile, our brain begin to feel more positive. Try it right now. Try to smile and be angry at the same time. If you truly embrace the smile, it is impossible to be angry at the same time.

Clowns have a reputation for putting a funny mask on their face and dressing up in ridiculous outfits. Yet, inside, they are very sad and negative. Psychologically, in using this method of smiling through your pain, you need to have a clear intention of why you are doing it. The idea is to create a mental environment to be humble and positive. I have experimented with this on myself. Yes, it took time for me to feel the smile and the happiness and the joy, but the point is, it worked.

When I smiled, I began to feel the joy of the smile. I wanted to feel happy so much so that I could overcome the feelings of frustration that were within me. So, if we are feeling down, or if we are ashamed of something that happened in the past, we can overcome it.

Decisions and Action

This is the first step to be in a basic transition mode. Just as we cannot teleport from A to B, we cannot make immediate changes in our lives by pushing a button. It would be a speculation if we lived in a Matrix, where we can plug into a computer and upload information, and say, "I learnt something." It would be merely a movie.

To Be Alive

I am in a wonderful place in life right now, but it has not always been this way. I have already shared part of my story; my life has not always been great. Regardless of where I was in my life, I followed my intuition, even when my ego was telling me otherwise.

When I was going through a difficult time involved in dangerous habits in my life, that created a platform for survival. I knew I needed to change in order to live a life I could enjoy.

At first, I tried to make positive changes in my life on my own. It took me 20 years to get to the point where I realised that I needed a mentor and coach; that was my next level. I had made a lot of progress by myself, but everything really began to fall into place when I started working with my mentor. Doing so helped me realise that we are all connected. I saw that I was not the only one who was trying to make positive changes in life. When I started my journey, I did not even know that what I was doing was called personal growth, personal development, and personal discovery. Now, I do.

The things that need to occur for you to achieve your goals (such as buying a home) start to appear in the world around us. However, if you are not engaged with your inner dialogue, and you are not taking steps toward your goal, what will happen? Nothing. Just like food, if we want to eat, we must go to the kitchen and prepare ourselves something, right? The same is true for our future, so, when you create your plan for the future, start moving toward your goal with both your thoughts and your actions.

CHAPTER FIVE

YOUR UNIQUE SELF-CARE

Fear of Failure

What is holding us back? What stops us from being our best? Is it the fear of failure? Just to let you know—failure does not exist. It is only a delay in our success. A lot of times, failure is simply not meeting a self-inflicted deadline we set for a target to be accomplished. But is this really failure?

It is possible that we did not have a balanced focus. We might have been so excited about something that we set an unrealistic timeframe. Or possibly, other factors entered the situation that caused us to re-prioritise or re-strategise our tasks. Completing the goal within the set period might not have been possible or realistic.

Fear is another element of life holding you back. However, fear is not the true source of what is holding you back from accomplishments. Fear can be replaced with knowledge. If you fear something, learn about it. Find out what you are afraid of. Once you feed yourself with knowledge about what you are afraid of, you can act. But ensure you are following medical advice from a professional and not trying to do it by yourself.

Shared Experiences

The past is, and always will be, our memory. Even if we have forgotten what happened, emotions are always with us. We cannot truly be rid of experiences from our childhood or adulthood. We may want to forget all about certain things, but guess what? We never forget.

If there is joy, the joy remains with us. If there is pain, the pain is there, but this doesn't mean we have to continue to endure the pain or discomfort from the past. It is possible to address the pain or frustration and treat it. It is never easy to create a replacement for our frustration, but it is entirely possible, no matter what.

Also, treating pain within us can be like travelling from one place to another. The trip may be long, but it is worth the journey. Why? Because it is a great story.

We all have negative emotions and feelings, but we are empowered to create unlimited possibilities to positively impact our life. Our ego might try to warn us that we cannot move on; that we can be safe in our comfort zone. But then we have tendencies to strive for more. The past is within us; the past is our present. This is a gift. It is a human aspect that allows us to grow continually and gradually.

Change and Motivation

Many people feel unmotivated. It may be because we do not know the future.

We tend to learn things that we believe are good for us. We learn, but we feel nothing about what we learn. There is no satisfaction or pride in our learning because we have no passion for learning the subject.

Therefore, we lose focus in learning what we are not really interested in. Without a specific plan, your interest in a subject, goal or even your true purpose can fall away. Since we cannot see how this will help us in the future, we might miss the opportunity. For this reason, keeping a clear vision of your future is important.

> *"You do not have to be psychic to know what you want*
> *for yourself and your family."*
>
> —Marki Spacilova

We might be uncertain about a lot of things. What would happen in the future if we lost our job, for example? Did we wait for it to happen, so we could have something to blame? Do we complain that it is not our fault? Do we let life happen to us?

In some cases, we are not in control of our life, and we are merely waiting for instructions on what to do. In this situation, there is no motivation. If we let life happen to us, how will we even be motivated enough to get out of bed?

There was a time when I was working as manager with a license to be allowed to sell alcohol, where we were selling wine. It was a typical English wine shop. One day, my friend asked me a very interesting question. She asked, "Are you going to do this job for the rest of your life?" I said, "I do not know. Right now, I am here, and when the time comes, I will know what to do." That is exactly what I said, and that is exactly what happened.

I stayed in that position, but I kept my eyes open for new opportunities. I didn't let life happen to me. I chose to take control of my life. When the time was right, I left that management position.

When I first left my job, I was couch-surfing with no fixed address, and I was in debt. Yet, I didn't give up. I took action, and a good job came my way. I had many jobs where I learned life lessons, and those life lessons have led me to become the author of this book, a spiritual entrepreneur, a spiritual life coach, business and productivity coach.

I'm now creating a platform of numerous possibilities to help people in need and also help the planet. I put myself into a dangerous situation by leaving my job. But in doing so, I found my path. While I was going through the transition, I kept saying to myself, "If I survive this, I will write a book about it. It may happen now or in five years." Well, since you're reading this now, you can see that my efforts to take charge of my life worked out well.

Self-Care

Challenge the fear: When you find fear in a challenge, ask yourself if your fear is caused by any of these four things.

There are four pillars of self-care:
- Self-esteem
- Self-confidence
- Positive approach
- Believing in yourself

Self-care comes with self-respect; this does not mean you are selfish. Taking care of ourselves first to build our self-esteem, self-confidence, positivity, and our belief in ourselves isn't a bad thing. When we take care of ourselves first, then we're able to help others.

On an air-plane, you must put on your own oxygen mask first before you can help others. Caring for yourself first is often the best thing you can do, because otherwise you're in no condition to be able to help others.

By the way, your self-esteem provides a spark for your self-confidence, which helps keep you moving forward.

Mindsets

We can make massive changes in our lives through self-conditioning. For example, I have been using self-talk to create an aversion to certain foods and drinks that I know are unhealthy for me. Through self-talk, I have conditioned myself to dislike the taste, and even smell, of sugary soft drinks because I know they are bad for me. In the same way, for foods that are good for me, I've trained my brain to adapt to enjoying the flavours of them. This technique has worked for me every time. Through discipline, I was able to change my mindset. I decided to use this process of changing my mindset for other things too.

It took me 21 days to upgrade my money mindset. I used to pay attention to marketing ploys like free samples or freebies. I bought items on sale that I didn't really need. Now, I think about circulating money. The more money you circulate, the more money will return to you. It is like Karma; what goes around comes around.

Changing your mindset is really about changing your habits, character, and life overall. Mindsets for discipline, focus, time management, motivation and self-care are some of the mindsets you want to grow.

Healing with a Strategy

I suffered from an unusual medical condition when I had unusual hiccups that lasted for over a year; doctors did not know how to help me. They prescribed some medication for me and told me I had irritation in my stomach, but there was no cure. I could not find a nutritionist or dietician to help me, so I made a decision to work on it myself.

I did an elimination diet. I started from scratch. I used a juicer to blend everything I ate. I started by introducing one food at a time. I cut out coffee in the morning, raw food, nuts, and eggs—everything.

Slowly, as I added one food at a time, I introduced all types of foods back into my diet over a period of two years. I began by searching for food and a type of cooking which did not cause me to hiccup. I maintained this food for one month, and then for the next month, I included another ingredient. It was not easy. Yet, my goal was to heal from the hiccups. Was I successful? Yes, I was.

Healing and Believing

For a long time, I suffered from Patellofemoral Pain Syndrome. I still do. However, I can manage my pain well now. What that means is that I have to avoid bending my knees at a sharp angle.

If I do this, I won't be able to stand up. Sitting in a lotus position during meditation is not possible for me. Just like with food and my hiccup situation, I created a plan for myself to improve my pain.

I also started to experiment with what exercises I could do. It was also part of observation and learning. It was a person-centred way to see how my body responded to my needs and wants. As I experimented with exercises, I changed from cycling to walking. I can tell you, for me, it was the best thing I could have ever done.

Cycling wasn't great for my knees. I realised I did not like cycling anyway. Cycling places was more about saving time and pilgrim travelling than anything else. Besides, I found that I love walking in nature and observing the life there. With the combination of the diet I found worked best for me and exercises, my health greatly improved.

At the start, I had a hard time believing I would lose my overweight, but with little actions over time, I was able to do it. I improved my life just because I learnt what my body needed, and then retrained myself to enjoy those foods even though I still wanted to eat food my body did not need any more.

CHAPTER SIX

RECONNECTING EMOTIONS AND FEELINGS

*"Do you like writing your thoughts? Writing might be
more important than you think."*

- Marki Spacilova

Gut Feelings

How can I motivate myself without anyone interfering? This question can be asked if you are ready to take a step you have been thinking about for a long time. It is like a nagging voice that says, "Just do it, just do it." This is about motivation coming to life.

Literally, what you think and how you act determine your future and who you will be. When motivation comes to life, our thoughts and actions can drive us forward. Life is so precious!

It is important to listen to that positive voice to "just do it." Likewise, we should also be wary of negative voices telling us to do something harmful. If you hear a voice telling you to harm yourself or another person, by all means avoid taking that type of action. In addition, seek professional help and please don't waste your time by playing video games, watching TV, and just having meaningless conversations that lead nowhere. Be motivated to do positive things.

Motivation starts with an idea. The idea will expand and will nag you and haunt you until you do something about it. Have you ever had a gut feeling that something is going to happen? That sensation comes from your digestive system. For example, you can feel "fear" in that area of the gut.

> *"If you are centred within yourself, you will become spiritually aware of yourself and your surroundings."*
>
> —Marki Spacilova

How can you get spiritually aware? There are many ways. One is as simple as eating food your body needs. The point is you need to make yourself feel lighter. For instance, junk foods make you feel sleepy and heavy. The lighter (healthy) the foods you eat, the more connected you will become within yourself.

Requirements for spiritual and emotional awareness:
- Lighter healthy food.
- Meditation or religious or cultural practices.
- Exercises.

Feelings and Being

There are many aspects of life we often tend to neglect. The main one is slowly letting ourselves get muted from spiritual intuition. We become distracted by constant social interactions, and we let governments and society control our lives. When this happens, we begin to miss the inner-spiritual guidance that is within us.

I found practising meditation, exercises and eating healthy food to be necessities for the start of my body's transformation. I chose to take control of my life. My perception of negativity began to improve right away, and for the first time in a long time, I felt excitement and enthusiasm. I felt alive!

I had to practise to maintain that feeling for as long as possible. It was not easy, but I was on a journey to feel happiness inside and out. We may feel disconnected or divided from society while not exactly knowing why, but in truth, it is not society we are disconnected from; we are disconnected from our own emotions and feelings.

Emotions

Emotions are peculiar; our brain and our gut feeling control them. There is a structure in the brain called the limbic system that was discovered in 1939. The term limbic system (from the Latin word Limbus which means edge) was first used in 1952. I found an experiment that shows how emotions work on the outside.

The experiment was about a child who was exposed to trauma (a rat and a noise) that shows how emotions are perceived. The scientists put a rat in front of the child, and everything was okay. However, when they repeated this - putting a rat in front of the child - while, at the same time, making a big boom sound behind the child, things were different. The child did not remember the big boom but remembered the rat. The child was more scared of the rat than the boom itself. In fact, the child did not even remember the big boom, but instead, remembered the rat and feared anything that even resembled the rat as well.

What I understand from this experiment; emotions are connected to the primal core of ourselves. It shows that we might not remember every detail of a past event. You may bring the memory to the surface, but you will also bring the memory of the emotion you do not want to feel. You may not know exactly what happened from every single angle. To truly understand the event, you would have to go back to the past to retrieve the information you had forgotten. If you decide to do so I recommend an NLP or hypnotherapy practitioner.

Once you can recognise your feelings, you are closer to connecting to your self-awareness. We may logically know our feelings, but more importantly, we need to connect the feelings with knowledge. If we do not do that, then we remain in a mental fog, and we are not in control of our lives because our emotions control us.

From Shakespeare, we can remember the line, "To be, or not to be, that is the question." I say, it is "to be." In the modern world, it is to exist or coexist with each other. There is a need to feel. It is enjoyable and soothing to be hugged and touched and feel that we are appreciated by others.

The first contact is the need to feel within ourselves. We cannot wait for someone else to truly help us feel one way or another. It is up to us to create positive emotions within ourselves. If we cannot feel it, we should try to become more in touch with our feelings.

Journalling and Scheduling

Journalling is a very good way to become more in touch with our feelings. We are often able to recognise things better while writing. However, it is not recommended to schedule too many tasks, as it will discourage you, making the overall process pointless.

Scheduling itself can be a type of journalling, just like adding things to your planner can also allow you to think through your tasks as you add them to your calendar. Some positive things to schedule might include adding a masterclass, webinar or training you wish to attend. You can add anything you feel you need to prioritise such as: appointments you have, going to work, breakfast, lunch, supper, and family time. Schedule free time too. Don't neglect this.

Make sure you have enough time between your activities to allow for travel time from one place to the next. Remember, you are starting small, so the actual deadline does not matter at the moment. You want to get used to doing the journalling and scheduling. As you get used to writing, journalling and scheduling, you can add more as you see fit.

Routines and Enthusiasm

When some people think of the word routine, they think boring. Some people don't like routines. These people will have a hard time to start one. They prefer to live more spontaneously. But come to think about it, being spontaneous has its price as well. While being spontaneous and having no structure, lifestyle can fluctuate, weight can fluctuate, and finances can fluctuate. That is not all, being spontaneous could mean having to be ready for whatever happens. On top of that, while living a life based only on spontaneity, we are not doing what we can, to plan for our future.

Having a routine, on the other hand, is structured. We know exactly what we want to achieve, and as a result, we can easily predict our future without even needing a psychic. We add repetition and patterns in our life. This repetition helps activate our memory. That means we start to remember more. We feel more alive than ever before. We are curious, and we want to try new things, new experiences, or adventures.

Feelings and emotions are activated; specifically, those we have not felt before. Having a routine provides us the comfort to be excited about our life. We can start feeling joy, excitement, and enthusiasm. Once we get used to a routine that becomes comfortable, then we can establish and expand more tasks.

Handwriting and Subconscious Thoughts

Handwriting is one skill that I used to be ashamed of. The way people write can determine what character and personality they have. This can also influence what we do. Paying attention to your handwriting can create a psychological discovery about yourself. With training, great handwriting can be achieved, and guess what? When your handwriting starts to improve and maybe even becomes artistic, then actual personality changes might occur as well.

Graphology: is the name given to the general subject of personality analysis, based on handwriting analysis. There are various schools of psychology – behaviourist, psychoanalytical, and so on — applicable to graphology. Handwriting could be called brain writing.

When you first began to form letters, you had to think about how to make each one of them; they were somewhat shaky at the start. I remember how difficult it was for me to form a sentence from all the letters and words. I had to test which hand was the prime writing hand. Are you left-handed or right-handed? When we first started learning how to write, we had to get used to it, and we got better at it with practice. Journalling is no different. We just need to get used to it as well. But after a while, your subconscious mind will begin to take over the duties of forming the letters.

Progress happens step by step with practice, and your subconscious begins to learn words. Then you have to only think about the meaning and the tasks you want to perform. And your subconscious mind sends electrical impulses to your hand, telling you how far to go for each stroke and how to make each letter within the word. Thus, you begin to write without conscious thought of the writing formation, and then it becomes automatic.

You become connected with the words. In other words, your brain or subconscious mind forms the characters as a result of habit. The pressure of your pen and the formation of each part of each letter shows your subconscious thinking. Which means you start creating a memory. Now that you have this information, it is easy to see how consciously changing your writing style through practice can lead to changes within your subconscious mind. The changes begin with transmuting negative habits into a positive way of living. Next comes the evolution of your character toward an ideal human being. The lasting result is the desire, by transformed people, to teach future generations.

CHAPTER SEVEN

CONNECTING SENSES TO
YOUR AWARENESS

"Have you ever tried to find the perfect technique for meditation?
To meditate, it does not matter if you put your hands up, down
or in a praying position. The result is the same."

– Anonymous

Consequence of Decision-Making

I have always been told to think before I speak or think before I act. In the past, I was impulsive in both of these areas, and I almost got into trouble for that. I am glad I survived to tell the story.

Our stories allow us to share experiences and lessons with others. Life is so precious! We can choose to create, build, or invent things to help others to follow the positive growth of their life. Anything is possible. We just must decide to do it.

Before we do anything, though, we need to know what we are doing — what are we focusing on? We can either choose to do everything or nothing; life will continue either way. But personally, I just thought if I do nothing, nobody will remember who Marki Spacilova was.

Realizing the importance of action is like a wake-up call. If we decide to create a platform for our lives, then we fulfil our duty to care and be alive. We upgrade our humanity to look after ourselves and our planet better. If everyone would think positively and exist harmoniously with everyone else, that would be paradise, would it not?

That is the ideology of the future. The negative way is to do nothing and just accept what we already have regardless of if we like it or not. Whereas the positive way is that human beings, with an open mind, can choose wisely and help others; we can teach the next generations how to live purposefully and productively.

Failure

Failure and setbacks are important. Why? They are our learning curve. We learn more when we feel the heaviness of failure on our shoulders. It is like a nagging feeling to do something about it. Whenever we encounter an obstacle or roadblock, we need to change direction or adjust the speed. Have you noticed that something you are doing is not working?

Mind, Body, and Spirit (According to the dictionary)

The mind is the element of a person that enables them to be aware of the world and their experiences, and to think and to feel; it is the faculty of consciousness and thought.

The body is full of neurons or specialised cells, transmitting nerve impulses and nerve cells. Each part has its own frequency like a radio. You can go to the cardiologist so they can listen to your heartbeat, or you can have an EEG and connect to a machine to monitor your brain activity.

Spirit is the non-physical part of a person; it is the seat of emotions and character — the soul.

Wouldn't it be great if we could connect to a machine to monitor activity of the spirit as well?

This is how I understand the spirit or the soul: Looking inwards can create an "aha" moment. We need to look deep within ourselves to realise that the answer to being content in life is learning that we are actually part of something much bigger.

We are, in fact, not alone. We are spirits with mind and body. We have an idea, but the same idea might be created by another person. Why? Because somehow, we are interconnected as one consciousness; all of us are connected. Have you ever felt like you were on the same frequency as someone else?

There are many anecdotes of people seeming to have telepathy with each other. For example, one person, maybe a mother, thinks of her daughter, and then the phone rings, and it is the daughter calling. Or a good friend senses that their friend needs to talk, calls them, and yes, the friend was experiencing some powerful emotion, and the call was timed perfectly. Things like this can happen because we are connected as one consciousness. We live individual lives, but we are never disconnected from everyone else.

Senses

Feelings and emotions are invisible, but we can sense them. How? Feelings are information. Our feelings such as anger, anxiety, depression, and hurt are hints that we are telling ourselves things that are untrue. We tend to treat ourselves in unloving ways out of habit. Our uncomfortable feelings around others can also be a sign that the other person is being judgemental, needy, angry, or inauthentic. But we cannot touch those feelings; we can only see them in the person's behaviour or how the person reacts. We might hear a person shout or raise their voice. We might feel a person if they become violent, but it is impossible to objectively see the actual energy of the anger.

Have you heard the expression "seeing is believing"?
When you stare into a camp-fire, and you see only the aura around the fire, how close can you get to the edge of the fire without burning your hand?

How far do you need to travel to see the multi-coloured flickers of the Northern Lights?
Where does the cloud have to be, so the sun hits it, creating a rainbow?
Yes, seeing is believing. Feeling is believing. Experiencing things is believing.

Intuition

The more we practise intuition, the more we will progress to it. The same is true about practising our talents to expand our abilities and passions. Our overall perception improves. That becomes noticeable on the outside by anyone who knows you. That's what we aim for.

Life Without All the Senses

We have at least five senses. We have sight, smell, taste, hearing and touch, right? What can we experience through our senses? In other words, what happens if we lose one of these senses, or are born without one? What would happen? We tend to ignore this possibility, and we take these precious connections within our body for granted.

When we meet someone who is blind, what do we do? Do we show humanity, gratitude, and respect with dignity? Or do we humiliate that person by acting weirdly because we know they cannot react?

Change

I remember there was a time when I was constantly complaining and moaning about things I did not like. I could go on and on about what was happening. Yet, I would do nothing about it. I would not act to change the situation. When people heard me complain, they always asked, "What are you going to do about it?" I always responded, "nothing."

People often decide that they will do nothing about things they complain about, and then they end up with more of whatever they do not like.

I noticed that each time I was complaining about something, I really meant that I did not know how to solve the situation. I did not act on those negative things because I felt I was not good enough to change them.

This is a serious, yet common reaction. We're actually scared of change. We do things that are not aligned with our journey in life. We tell ourselves there is nothing else for us. We also tell ourselves that not changing is safe, yet we complain about it.

The Sense of Intuition

A good start for change is using our intuition and transforming it into awareness. It is time to change your perception on awareness. When we know when we are not happy, we tend to avoid the situation and seek something we think is better. We avoid solving the situation, and in the process, settle for less just to feel comfortable. This creates a vicious cycle; one where we do not know that we could do more and be productive. Instead, we just go in circles.

Example: Someone chooses an excellent employer they want to work for. But then, they end up changing jobs. They leave the good employer because there are other employees and obstacles in the workplace. A change was made, yes. However, the action of the change removed the person from what might have been a good position to be in. Would you feel better if you found a solution to the root of the problems in the workplace? Change them instead of running from them to find a new job. The chances are the next job will have the same problems. How long does the cycle need to continue? The better way might not require leaving the job. Rather, it is a lesson about upgrading our self-awareness, and finding out why we are at the job in the first place. What could change to make us happy to stay? What might we learn by staying there?

Imagination

When we understand the knowledge we learnt, we become wiser, and then our confidence grows. We can also choose to share the knowledge with others. In the same vein, we can study subjects that seem interesting, but may not remember what we've learnt. If this is happening to you, you might want to ask yourself if what you are studying truly aligns with your purpose.

It seems that when we study things that are in alignment with our purpose, we retain the knowledge easily. When we study things that do not align with our core values and goals, the opposite is often true.

You absorb information easily when you have an interest in meaningful to you that is central to you. Furthermore, when you study things that align with you, you become passionate about the subject. Your memory and creativity increase automatically.

Visualisation

Before anything is manifested in the physical form, it is formed in our minds. This is what the power of visualisation does. Before a vision has become reality you already feel it, see it and can believe in it. You use all your senses you have at your disposal. Alongside visualisation, you can also pray or meditate.

To make positive changes within yourself, you can also use affirmations, quotes you find meaningful, or just a psalm or a verse from a religious book. No matter the perspective or angle you take to examine the issue at hand, the results are the same. The results are always there. These types of journeys allow our senses to help create passion and positive changes in our lives. This is a person-centred form of growth. Your journey begun as soon as you began reading this book. Your perception of life has already changed. What will you choose to visualise next?

CHAPTER EIGHT

TUNING INTO FORGIVENESS AND MAKING AMENDS

"Creating good vibes and good feelings is important
because feeling good is instant happiness."

—Marki Spacilova

Avoiding vs. Solving Conflict

Most people want to be free from disagreement. When there is conflict with family or friends, we tend to separate from them, just to have peace of mind; but this can cause bigger problems than we think. Once we separate from a family member or friend, we can never be sure if we will ever see them again. It forces us to decide how important it is to stay away from them or if it is better to try to amend the relationship.

We can start by forgiving or learning to forgive. Like any conflict, there are opportunities in lessons. We may experience setbacks along the way, but continuing to move forward will actually help to heal someone or even heal ourselves. Life comes with challenges. One of the best ways to create a lesson from a challenge is to step out of our comfort zone and face our inner shadows.

Coming Back to Life

While you are working towards aligning your spiritual and physical world, you can do whatever it takes to gain more confidence in the subject that is most important to you; the subject you want to practise for the rest of your life. Also, if you had any trauma in the past, trust is part of the healing process.

Before me, other notable people have talked about trust, confidence, and self-esteem; they went through the process as well. But personally, I found out that I like to focus on the time line of the past, present, and future.

> *"I trust myself first, and I am confident that what I am saying is true. I have found that I have to trust my intuition, gut feeling or sixth sense. Only then, am I able to trust others."*
>
> —Marki Spacilova

Many business owners and tradespeople have made something big from nothing, including myself. There was a time when I was lost, and I even visited the mental health department to get help processing traumatic experiences. Why?

My story: One day, while I was on duty, I was held hostage in the off licence (wine shop) during a robbery. While I was being held hostage in the shop, I was more heroic than anyone could imagine. The robbers nearly killed me by strangling me. But for some reason, I was meant to survive that ordeal, and I did survive. Eventually, those robbers were arrested.

But what happened to me? I lost my way and struggled for nearly two years. I found myself on the streets, in debt. Luckily, I had a core value within myself that did not allow me to take my own life. Instead, I chose to seek help. I had an urge to survive, and it was stronger than what I was against.

This crisis allowed me to see exactly what was important to me. I found a way to "come back to life," and that's why this book is titled Come Back to Life. Maybe you are in a similar situation as I was? Maybe you feel lost? If so, let these words be a glimmer of hope because I am living proof that it is possible to go from being lost in life to coming back to life. If the business owners who struggled before me and I can bounce back to life with confidence, you can do it too.

Learn the History of Your Parents

Before we are born, many have come before us. Those people had a unique history and lessons to learn as well. The way they learnt things was completely different from how you are learning right now.

Imagine the brain capacity and acceptance of life during World War II. People of this era thought differently from people of the current world. This is only one example where people had different things that they had to consider in life. Every era has specific things they need to address, and thus, every era is different. But then, there are things that can overlap between generations.

When I was born I was still affected by the era of the 60s or 70s and the hippie era. Take music as an example. I like the music from ABBA and Queen or even the Beatles. Despite that these bands were popular long before I was born. I enjoy the sound and influence of this music from a prior era. It is not my era, but I still accept its influences.

Stages of Life and the Reasons to Make Amends

A person-centred approach to listening to your own body, mind and spirit is when you notice your family and friends might have a different perspective on life.

Most people suffer from some form of health problem, and when it comes to our parents, some might even have brain disease.

What is so special about our brain?

Well, for one, our brain is the main control centre of our living body, and like a computer, our brain can be enhanced. Brain enhancement is the process of developing innate abilities that allow you to retain memory. When you retain memory, you function better in the society, at your workplace, in the home, and so on. The brain is a unique organ that produces thoughts and feelings. It also includes the anatomy that controls the centre of your nervous system.

Stages of Life and Awakening

Childhood development is considered from zero to 10 years old. During this time, the child learns to walk, talk, accept and reject things. A lot happens, from first falls to standing up, to learning how to interact with others.

The next life stage is adolescence, which spans the ages of 11 to 19. At this developmental stage, they are getting a much deeper understanding of concepts like love. Concepts like taking care of themselves, developing specific tastes for food they like to eat and learning more about acceptance and rejection also begin to form in their minds.

Psychology has provided a list of different attributes to track developmental stages based on age. Some children might have an IQ that is higher than other children in their current developmental stage. For example, late adolescence is normally listed as between the ages 16 and 19, however, for me, it lasted until the age of 25 years.

The shift out to adolescence is the first attempt at real independence, separating from parents and wanting to be self-determining. The turmoil of ups and downs, and the reflection of what was learnt and forgotten is doubled, and often comes to the surface.

From a spiritual perspective: What I learnt from my research and experience and personal testing - We can draw from the Hindu term Kundalini. This is a form of divine energy. Once Kundalini is activated, it is hard to control. The name itself is from Sanskrit, meaning "coiled snake." However, there really is a way to control it when it starts. One way to do this is to find a Kundalini yoga expert to help channel this electric energy of awakening.

From a psychological perspective: Adulthood may begin from the age of 20 or 21, but if for some - just like it was with me - adolescence is still in place until the age of 25, they might feel disconnected from themselves. This can cause mental health problems and feelings of being lost. The good news is that you don't have to remain in this state. Help is there, and all you need is assistance from a trained registered professional who can guide you through this time.

Learning to Forgive

There is a big difference between forgiveness and forgetting. Learning how to forgive is a skill learnt through life experience. It is also one of the best skills a person can learn. Nobody can explain the magical power of true forgiveness to you. This is something you need to experience for yourself. Forgiveness is different than forgetting.

Once you understand the history of your past and the past of your ancestors, then you can have the necessary knowledge and wisdom to forgive. You can learn to forgive yourself for holding grudges against people who might have had different opinions or a different life-vision than you. Forgiving others and yourself is a liberating thing that can help us positively move to new stages in life.

Before You Know It

In extreme - but not uncommon - cases, dementia can happen to anyone. A parent living with dementia may have forgotten you are their son or daughter by the time you decide to make amends with them. Imagine how painful that might be if you avoided them for months, or even years. Now, they are living with dementia. Wouldn't you prefer to make amends before anything like could happen? That way, after you make amends you will have time to create new memories with your parent to replace the hurt from the past. Well, once the dementia sets in, this might not be possible.

Also, what if someone dies before they could even enjoy their retirement, or worse, enjoy a good conversation with their son or daughter. This is painful to think about, but those thoughts might encourage you to make amends if there is a conflict between you and another person. You might even want to forgive them if you must. This is to create the closure you need to move on or to let go for yourself.

"No matter how you see it, forgiveness might be the most powerful antidote to the bad feelings you have about the people you hold a grudge against."
—Marki Spacilova

Your parents probably raised you the best way they knew how; nobody is perfect. They did it because they believed this was the right way for your upbringing. You may not agree with me right now, because your family was mean, aggressive, or even so violent that you had to run away. That may be true, but ask yourself this: Are they the same now or have they changed?

Forgiveness might still be a cure. As a person of higher awareness, you can forgive someone even if they have not changed. You can detach yourself from the memory and forgive them. Doing this will benefit your inner peace on an energetic level, and the people whom you forgive will feel it too.

"Sometimes, we feel as if we've failed when we don't get what we want straight away."
—Marki Spacilova

Achieving Positive Self-Talk

Having a job where you follow policies, regulations and procedures could be safe and rewarding. You meet lots of people, and you learn about life. But you may feel there is more to life than what you are doing. When this happens, it can feel like your world is upside down. At a certain age, you may think you've done nothing which involves money, energy, effort, time and life itself. At the age of 40, you realise you have not accomplished anything, and time is running out — or is it?

Each generation of humans lives longer, such that today, living up to 100 years is not all that uncommon. When we reach a certain age, we think we are too old to study. This is a dangerous way to think. Be open-minded and realise that there is always going to be more to learn and do.

> *"Live as if you were to die tomorrow. Learn as if you were to live forever."*
> - Mahatma Gandhi

I can tell you, thinking you are too old or too young to do something is debilitating; by so doing, you tell yourself you do not want to learn. If you do this, your brain will not be able to process everything you want to learn. You are programming your brain not to retain things you might want to learn for self-development or even for your job. We limit ourselves with self-talk such as, "I am too old (or too young) for this." However, age does not have a direct connection with ability. How can you change your mindset?

Fun fact: People come into our lives to teach us lessons.

CHAPTER NINE

CREATING A PLEASANT ENVIRONMENT IN YOUR WORKPLACE, NO MATTER WHAT

Learn to Expand Your Mind, Body, and Spirit

The outcome of every situation in the workplace starts with you. It is about your brain capacity and how you handle stress on a daily basis. You see, the brain is complex. As much as I want to understand it fully, there is always another aspect or part of the brain to be explored. As humans, in the process of getting older, we can choose to learn as much as we want. But what happens when we start improving our mind, body, and spirit?

Personally, I used to suffer from migraines. I could not handle any stress because of the capacity of my brain. Any stress or condition of working under pressure would give me migraines.

I saw progress from my learning, and I wanted to continue improving my situation, so I developed a healthier way of living. I began coping with daily stresses as well. I still experienced burnout from time to time, but I eliminated the debilitating migraines. My life became filled with experiences and life lessons that gave me courage.

Even in times when I felt lazy, I still managed to exercise. Even if I wanted to eat junk food, I would still choose healthy foods to eat.

Consequently, I became wiser and more observant. I learnt to observe the behaviour of people around me. I learnt many types of exercises and meditations. Eventually, I chose to adapt and use whatever was required to deal with stress or high levels of pressure. I did a complete health makeover. I did a complete revision of how I was eating and taking care of myself. By doing all of this, I became confident that I could be a student and a teacher at the same time.

You see, if you are diligent, you will be able to become aware of your mind, body, and spirit too. You can be a teacher and a student. Our own self-improvement can happen even faster when we teach someone else what we have learnt. This is the higher principle of sharing. Have you heard the expression, "Sharing is caring"? I believe this to be true.

Create a Job within a Job even as a tradesperson or business owner

You may be employed and not like your current workplace or your boss. Personally, I have never left any job because I had a problem with management or a member of the staff. However, I have left a job because I felt I could better contribute my skills, talents and abilities elsewhere for the greater good.

Have you ever considered creating a job within a job? There is a step-by-step system to level up and progress in what you love to do. Some workplaces may be challenging because of management differences of opinion or a member of staff who may not like you for some unknown reason. Even with a situation like this, I don't think quitting is the best option because there will always be other challenges in other jobs. It is wiser to focus on finding your own place and making the situation better in the job you already have. After all, there is a reason you got that job in the first place.

Complaining or running away from a difficult job will only create a pattern of one bad job after another. If you want to break the pattern, you need to stand up to find a way to appreciate your current job by making it meaningful to you. This is much better than just going to the next job without changing anything.

> *"Being the CEO of your own life is a skill that you can develop. However, you can also take the opportunity to learn from a toxic workplace and not allow yourself to be affected by the influences of the work environment which means mastering your precious life."*
>
> - Marki Spacilova

Upgrade Your Confidence

I have noticed that changes create confidence. Even if I am not good at the new skills I am trying to learn from the start, consistency is key in developing a new habit. Something as simple as sitting upright in a chair can make positive changes in your confidence (and posture). When I started this practice during meditation, in my first month, I was not consistent. However, with repetition, I learnt how to consistently do this. The result was that I gained self-esteem. I learned how to implement what I learnt in my life. Knowledge is powerful, but, if we do not use knowledge in our own life, then the knowledge is worthless.

There is a saying, "When you do not use it, you will lose it." I heard that from a doctor who was talking to an elderly person who was refusing to walk. Not walking was the elderly person's choice. However, by not walking over time, they were at risk of losing the physical ability to walk. This can happen to anyone.

I encourage you to incorporate what you learn into your lifestyle or way of life. If you don't use what you learn, you will lose it. But, if you implement what you learn, you will see progress from the beginning to the end.

There is a saying that expresses this well:
"I can bring a horse to the pond to drink, but it is up to the horse to drink the water."

There is no end to self-learning. If you can learn to accept yourself, you will notice that what you tell yourself matches your way of living. When this happens, it is valid to say, "I am good enough." And the process of self-acceptance and self-learning never ends. What I do not know, I will learn. What do I need to learn?

Fill your mind with the things you want to learn and the things you want to have as part of your life. If you do this, your thoughts will be manifested in your physical reality. If you are focused on spirituality, then automatically, it becomes a reality. The multidimensional spirituality can be manifested in the physical world. This does not have to happen straight away; it takes time to build.

Upgrade Your Self-esteem

Self-esteem, self-worth and self-care are the qualities of a transcended business leader. This is because self-esteem is your ability to be successful in whatever you put your mind to. Self-worth offers you the privilege of being a student and a teacher at the same time. Do you remember what you have experienced in your life? What did you learn? What can you share with like-minded people? Do you feel proud of yourself?

If you've learnt something and shared it, that's an achievement. Why? Because both of you are gaining knowledge and helping each other to gain knowledge to continue. It means you have all the abilities you need to have self-respect and self-confidence. It does not matter what someone thinks about you either. The most important thing is how you feel about yourself after accomplishing things in your life.

Mastering your past, present and future is key to fulfilling your purpose as well. When you think about mastering your past, then you have learnt from the good and the bad experiences. You have accepted them all as equally important. How can you utilise those experiences? Learning, in your present moment, for the purpose of positively impacting your future is important, because the present moment is the main source of change for the direction of your life.

Having said this, I have found that the most enlightened future is all about forgiveness and peace. It is also about the self-respect you gain from your past experiences. When you master your present moment, you know the importance of self-care, self-esteem, and self-worth.

CHAPTER TEN

BECOMING A UNITED TRANSCENDED BUSINESS LEADER

What Is Your Divine Call?

For many, creating their own company is almost like a calling. What happens if you hear this voice? What happens when you follow the divine call? It is difficult to totally separate the spiritual from anything we do, including work.

Whether we like it or not, we all have a purpose. We can choose to either accept our purpose on Planet Earth or not. If you accept, you will most likely attract like-minded people to work with you. These people might be your clients, your teammates, and/or your business partners.

These people might come from any background, culture, or religion. When you find the right people surrounding you, rest assured that you have listened to your intuition — your inner wisdom. You've listened to your passion, and let it guide you.

What Does It Mean to Be a Transcended Business Leader?

Being a transcended business leader means you accept people no matter who they are, irrespective of the culture or ethnicity they come from or the religion they follow. It also means accepting yourself regardless of what you have done in your past or what has happened to you.

As a transcended business leader, you accept differences between like-minded people and even those who think differently; you treat all people with gratitude, respect, dignity, equality, and inclusion.

Consider all the possibilities. You can use your wisdom and power to think of ways to help people who are from poor or disadvantaged backgrounds through technology or collaboration with others. What can you do to help them meet the bare necessities of food, water, clothing, and shelter? You can create an environment where they are provided assistance, so they don't even need to ask for help. Provide them with a healthy environment, so they can take care of themselves.

This role is not restricted to the responsibility of helping like-minded people and Planet Earth. It is about uniting business owners, tradespeople and leaders who are willing to put aside any limiting beliefs from their environment and culture. You can truly become a "light-worker" by answering the divine call.

United Transcended Business Leader

Why is uniting people globally important?
This modern era is heading toward uniting people globally, and collaboration is a brilliant opportunity to connect with people from around the world.

Collaboration is very unique and vital when it comes to any relationship, whether professional, personal, or even spiritual. Uniting business owners or tradespeople is a new trend, which is better than being business rivals who only compete with each other's products or services.

Rather than sticking with the old paradigm of competition in business, it is much easier, and more beneficial, for all parties involved to combine forces. Regardless of if it is a small business, a medium business or a large organisation, cooperation is possible.

These days, some businesses are no longer sustainable because of the lack of adaptation to new situations and lack of collaboration with other businesses. These businesses are replaced, as new businesses emerge. Sometimes, we need to let go of the old and welcome the new. Partnerships can range from sharing an entire brand or merely co-marketing on a small project.

> *"Persistent thinking and brainstorming can help you to develop business relationships and partnerships that could lead to an enormous empire of united transcended business leaders. These leaders could be just the change that will help Planet Earth become a better place."*
>
> —Marki Spacilova

The Importance of Understanding Your Type of Business

Understanding the character required for your business is crucial. You need to have certain skills, talents, and abilities. When you are working in an area of your expertise, you need to be focused. It is not about just going from A to B, there is a whole journey involved.

Completing this journey is not only based on faith and hope; it is more about understanding what your purpose is and what you are all about. When you know your talents, and you are creative, you can accomplish anything, including opening the business you are meant to have. In order to stay on track, you need to be sure of what you are doing on a daily basis. It is ideal to have a daily structure and create a healthy routine.

Creating productive days is important. Once you organise your day in a way that you have productive days, those productive days will turn into productive months, and then, productive years. More so, age does not matter in this process. Creating productive days that turn into productive weeks, months and years produces the same results regardless of if you are young or old. Either way, you are increasing your knowledge and deepening your expertise through your productive time.

Regardless of what your purpose is, you cannot accomplish your dreams without your active participation. You need to look after yourself too. Self-care is very important in business. As stated earlier, exercise is extremely important. Whether it is chi-gong, yoga, or any type of fitness you prefer.

Exercise is important. Meditation or prayer is also important, alongside a healthy diet. Hopefully, while reading this book, you've already began these things. How do you feel so far? If you are exercising, meditating, or practising religion and eating healthily, you are most likely maintaining a good balance of chemistry in your body and your emotional state of being (If you have started doing these things, make sure you have done so under supervision of an appropriate registered professional.).

Repetition is key. It doesn't matter if you diet for ten days or a month. If you go back to the same old habits, it will not work. You have to be consistent; when you're consistent, you will form healthy habits, which will in turn will lead to refined behaviour and character. It also increases self-awareness, as you will know exactly what you can or cannot do.

Your desire has to be part of your character. You have to practise everything we've discussed in order to progress.

The Importance of Meeting New People

As I already mentioned, networking and knowing the right people is important. It is good to support others and have support from others. Have you heard the acronym YANA? YANA—you are not alone. Because you are not alone, you are probably already being mentored, coached, and helped to come back to life. With mentoring and coaching, you see the value of your talents and continue to develop them.

Passion can transform into your purpose, and your purpose leads to a fulfilled life. When we are fulfilled, we are able to focus on what is important. What you want is not the same as what you need. Working with others can help you see the difference between what you need and what you want. Brainstorming is one great way to work together to generate ideas on what is important. Other ways include creating a member's club or a group of people who will be part of your project.

Being an Employee

An employee is really anyone who accepts a daily, weekly, biweekly, or monthly salary. I believe employees have to listen to their employer and follow instructions. When you agree to the job you are applying for, you are accepting the salary which is offered; you are also accepting the conditions and rules that come with the job. I know some people want more money and complain that their income is not enough. May I remind these people that they signed the contract and agreed to the salary? That's what happens when you are an employee. The tasks, rules, procedures, and policies may change over time with company updates and evolving technologies. Often, more tasks are given without additional pay. Still, in the end, it is your choice to work as an employee or not.

You Are Enough to Be a Transcended Business Leader

Considering what you have learnt so far, how do you feel? If you followed the advice in earlier chapters, you have been journalling since the beginning of this book. By now, you might have enough content to write your own book. Why not? You are the CEO of your own life now. You know that you can start or upgrade your business and become a tradesperson, business owner or united transcended business leader if you follow your calling with passion and planning. If you haven't done it yet, take the next step to become an owner, founder, or business partner. You can do it. But never start your business alone. Always seek help from a trained expert.

Practising being the CEO of your life is a great way to train to become a transcended business leader. There is only the additional paperwork, planning and legal obligations left to take care of. Before you progress to register as self-employed, you have to consider all the options in business to become a tradesperson/business owner/founder entrepreneur/partner. If you did not start your business yet then try to get help while doing it. You need to be surrounded by like-minded people, so you can feel supported. There is a difference between being a business owner and being a united transcended business leader. You can continue to make progress through a step-by-step system to upgrade and evolve.

If you are already a business owner, entrepreneur or tradesperson and this book inspired you to become much more, then you can become a united transcended business leader.

A united transcended business leader is concerned with more than just themselves and their business; they are also concerned about others and Planet Earth. More so, they don't see other businesses as the competition. They are in harmony and unity with others, and their priority is to live in a sustainable and eco-friendly way in their personal life, family life, business and any other facet of life they choose.

Being a united transcended business leader isn't necessarily easy, but the rewards are great. As a united transcended business leader, you can accomplish anything you want to accomplish while following your true inner purpose. You can also make a difference by helping others.

Did You Enjoy This Book?

Are you a person with the conviction, energy and potential to take your life opportunities to the next level by creating future and untold possibilities by working to implement all of its book's contents in tandem with Marki Spacilova? Self-belief is a MUST. Please, share your feedback from the site where you purchased the book. Thank you.

COMPANION EXERCISE BOOK

"These are disciplined and carefully planned exercises. It is ultimately your decision and responsibility to elect how you are going to utilise them in the most beneficial way for you. Any registered professional you choose to collaborate with in the future to assist you with your future plans may wish to consult with the author prior to commence. Please be sure to follow the disclaimer, warranty, and liability details at the start of the book."

—Marki Spacilova

5 Tips to Optimise These Exercises

Tip 1: Choose wisely

Read carefully the book chapters along with the exercises.

Use a word.doc or notebook to write your notes accompany your reading.

Create your questions and answers for the coach.

Create your questions and answers for each subject.

Research.

Commitment, consistency, courage and the desire to become a CEO is a MUST.

Progress step by step gracefully, steadily and with a final goal in mind.

Request a discovery call with the author, Marki Spacilova.

Tip 2: Using this guide will also help you to establish:

Who you truly are.

What you are really capable of.

What is your true purpose in your working life.

How can you empower yourself?

Tip 3: Use the model in each chapter to see where you can challenge yourself and where you can change your approach to life.

Meet Ali: Example questions to ask yourself:

Money - How much money would you like to earn?

Energy - How do you want to feel every day?

Effort - How productive do you want to be daily?

Time - When do you want to take control of your life?

And - Who do you trust enough to include them in your life including expertise from registered professionals?

Life - What sort of life do you want to lead?

Itself - What do you believe in?

Tip 4: Don't aim for perfection

Remember, every beginning has a start. A flower does not grow from a seed in one day.

The author does not want you to be overwhelmed at first reading. This is all about collaboration with the right people for you.

Go easy on yourself.

Learn from your mistakes once you become aware of them. None of us learns from success alone.

Tip 5: Team up with the Author Marki Spacilova

Please be open-minded to the possibility of undertaking these exercises with any relevant or appropriate expert in a competing field but be wary as to checking their professional standards and qualifications before establishing any formal working relationship.

If you are finding the process exciting, share your progress by way of a feedback loop.

Contact Marki if you feel you are ready to join the community for transcended business leaders.

Marki looks forward to hearing from YOU if you want to partner to create and build a viable community together.

Chapter 1: Turning Negative Experiences into Positive Lessons

First, ask the right open questions.

For example:

What did you learn about the event; i.e., the negative situation?

How would you do it differently now or next time?

The principle of the past technique:

This is what you can do when you see it in the present moment.

Randomly pick a memory and create questions around it.

Bring it into the present moment.

At that point, extract the lesson learnt.

Find a pattern.

Avoid repeating the same pattern.

When you get into a similar situation again, this time, you know better.

(Seek help from a NLP practitioner or hypnotherapist.)

The principle of the future technique:

This is when you understand the principle of the past technique.

Recall your negative experiences as life lessons.

Observe the opportunity to do something about it.

Create the possibility for your future accordingly.

Understanding the principles of the past and present is key to understanding the principle of the future.

The principle of the present moment:

If we do not understand our life lessons in the present moment, we will not know what the future will be like.

Life itself will become stagnant.

We will not understand why certain circumstances repeat themselves.

We will always enter new negative situations.

We will become ill and not take any action to cure ourselves.

This is when you understand your lessons in the present moment.

You take control of your past and your future at the same time.

You continue your step-by-step progress with clarity.

You adapt to new circumstances with ease.

"If you choose to combine helping like-minded people and creating an eco-friendly and sustainable business, you will become a united transcended business leader yourself."

—Marki Spacilova

Chapter 2: Discovering What Prevents You from Taking Action

Fear

Remember that fear needs to be fed with knowledge.

Find out what you are afraid of and learn it. (Seek help from a psychologist or therapist.)

Use the lesson to your advantage.

Re-purpose your findings.

Money:

Create a suitable budget. (Seek help from a registered financial advisor or equivalent professional.)

Set up a savings account and transfer 10% of your salary into the saving account of your choice every month.

Do not touch the money from your saving account until you have saved 6-months' worth of your salary.

Set up your own rule for using your savings.

If you are pursuing a goal, there are questions you ought to ask yourself to be sure that you are on a good path.

The first closed questions are:

Do I like what I am learning?

Is it easy for me to learn it?

If the answer is yes, then the subject is probably right for you.

But if the answer is no, you might want to look more deeply into whether the subject is perfect for you.

If it is a situation where you must learn something just because someone says so, there are two options: Be smart enough to avoid the subject altogether.

If it is something that must be learned to complete a task: You can employ someone else to do it for you.

To stay focused: the recommendation is to choose five things you want to do every day.

An ideal guideline for your daily routine should include:
Three things about your family and children. (Seek help from your significant other/parents psychologist or therapist.)
One thing about your interest and everything about you in the present moment.
One thing you want to do in the future.
And then... just do it!
Where do you want to be?
1-year vision.
5-year vision.
20-year ahead vision.
Sound difficult? Trust me, the hardest part is the beginning. Once you begin, the rest is easy-peasy.

Chapter 3: Creating Change in Your Life

This time you are going deeper:
Find out about the detailed step-by-step progress.
What do you need in each category to M.E.E.T. A.L.I.?
Set up a reasonable deadline for each category.

Don't give up if you fail your deadline.

Re-evaluate and start again.

Follow up on chapters 1 and 2.

Ask yourself: What do you want to happen in your life?

An example of a bucket list:

Tip

Always question why you want it.

A healthy family.

A house with a garden.

A thriving private and professional life.

The ability to travel.

Meeting new people.

All of the above.

The list must be written with passion:

You must feel it.

Envision it.

Imagine living the life you desire.

You need to be intentional about adopting it into your thoughts.

Talk about it with your family and friends.

Learning and Support from Others

The best ways to have a fulfilled life is:

Study.

Practice.

Become an expert in your industry.

Deepen your talents and abilities.

Your mission must be important.

Collaboration with registered professionals in their field of expertise must be a part of your life.

Improve your chances of success.

Include like-minded people who will help you to transform your life.

What can you do to free yourself from this situation:

Start with small steps.

Choose to slowly reduce the time you are spending on unwanted activities.

At the same time, increase the time doing more constructive things like studying.

Remember small steps.

Step-by-step progress.

Start with research.

Start by asking questions such as, how can I motivate myself?

Chapter 4: Motivation from Within

What to do if the goal is too big?

Think big. Yes.

Extend the timeline of your progress? Yes.

Structure each section:

Beginning details - Middle details - Ending details.

There is a process to go through in each section:

You will need to talk to the right people.

You need the finances for it.

Ensure you do not miss anything.

When there is a missing link, then the whole plan can be paused or stopped.

There are three simple things you need to do:

Decide - Act - Know why you want to make a change.

Ask these questions:

Am I in a place in life I do not enjoy?

Do I want to stay in that mode?

Now, decide to choose to change what you do not like.

How to use the law of attraction in your case:

Have very intentional thoughts and affirmations about what you want to accomplish.

Set up a step-by-step plan.

Map it out visually.

Action it.

What to do if you find yourself procrastinating:

Find out the reason(s) behind it.

See if there is a lesson for you there.

How to use the smiling technique:

Practice smiling at others even if you don't feel happy inside.

Start to modify your feelings and behaviour too.

The intention of the smile must be positive.

You must let the positivity radiate.

You don't have to dress up as a clown.

Please note:

A big smile can go a long way in creating positivity around and within you.

Position in life:

Continue to progress step-by-step.

Attain financial freedom and abundance.

Have true joy in your life.

Desire to have a healthy professional and family life.

Be happy inside and out.

Achieve this by taking the journey.

Tell your story of how you did it.

Chapter 5: Your Unique Self

Create a daily routine:

What foods can you eat without having a bad reaction? (Seek help from a Dietitian or Nutritionist.)

What exercises do you enjoy doing? (Seek help from a Physiotherapist or equivalent profession.)

Find out what motivates you.

What can you do to be productive daily? (Seek help from the Author Marki Spacilova.)

When do you need to go to sleep? (Seek help from a sleep doctor.)

When do you need to get up? (Seek help from a sleep doctor.)

Find out what is not working in your life.

Use the right questions, such as Why?

What are your values?

Learning from Failure

Ask yourself questions such as:

What did you learn from it?

Could you have done something better?

Do you need help from someone else to process?

Am I afraid of continuing?

Am I ready to take the next step?

Am I willing to move forward?

Rethink what you can do to move forward:

Think about why you did not meet your goals on time.

Stop resentment and doubt.

Replace it with a solution.

Re-evaluate your goals.

It is also important to look at the big picture.

Take the time to decide what you want to accomplish in your life.

Set up your priorities.

Set up a realistic timeframe.

Realize it is not a failure but a life lesson.

Change the direction where necessary.

Shift your focus on your priorities.

Accept the delay as a lesson in life.

Questions you can ask yourself:

How about you?

What will happen to you?

What will you choose to do for yourself?

Are you motivated?

If there is nothing to give you motivation, how can you motivate yourself?

Is it even possible to get motivated without anyone to help you?

Ask yourself:

Do you lack self-esteem?

Do you lack self-confidence?

Have you stopped being positive?

Have you stopped believing in yourself? (Seek help from a registered health professional.)

How to pursue your goal:

Have you stopped to see if it is really for you, or if you're doing it for someone else? As we begin to transform ourselves, it is important that, as we mature in our growth, we continually evaluate the "why" of our actions.

Why are you pursuing your goal?

Start believing in yourself.

Respect what you believe in.

Develop your positive approach.

Make it valuable for others.

Make it valuable for you.

Understand what you are doing.

Believe that this is the right thing to do.

Create unshakable self-esteem.

> *"If you are centred within yourself, you will become spiritually aware of yourself and your surroundings."*
>
> —Marki Spacilova

Chapter 6: Reconnecting Emotions and Feelings

The feelings are easily named:

Anger.

Frustration.

Disappointment.

Sadness.

Recognise your feelings and ask these questions:

Can you feel them?

Can you understand which one is which?

How many feelings do you experience regularly?

Recommendation:

(Seek professional medical assistance when required.)

Write them down.

Write down the feelings you can sense right now.

Connect emotions and feelings with:

Negative past experiences.

Positive past experiences.

Negative present moment experiences.

Positive present moment experiences.

Questions for the future experiences:

What do you want to experience in the future and why?

Who do you want to meet with in the future and why?

What do you want to contribute to your community and why?

How do you want to make a difference for the next generations?

Why?

What emotions and feelings will you expect in your life in the future and why?

Process of journalling and scheduling:

Start small.

Find a journal that is suitable for you.

There are so many journalling resources out there such as planners, calendars, diaries and so on; choose one.

Decide which one would be easy for you to maintain.

Make sure you have enough space for your writing too.

Write down your thoughts.

Schedule your morning routine.

Create your writing habit to journal about your thoughts.

Chapter 7: Connecting Senses to Your Awareness

What to do when you become self-aware:

Learn a person-centred approach.

Be authentic.

Apply what you learnt.

Measure the learning from your own experience.

Be sure to understand what you learnt from the experiences.

Acknowledge how you feel about it.

When you achieve that, celebrate!

Accept that the situation that did not work out for you was not a sign of failure.

Create a lesson from failure instead.

It might also be a life lesson you cannot learn in school or university.

What happens when you feel confident?

Self-esteem is higher.

Self-esteem and confidence are more obvious in the way we talk.

With this self-esteem, we become positive.

We become eager to continue to make progress.

Write down your thoughts:

How do you feel?

What did you experience through this journey so far?

You can sense your progress with:

Touch - Hearing - Smell - Sight - Feeling.

Ability to upgrade your senses to a much higher level.

Ability to use all the five senses channelled through inner wisdom.

Use your preferred method (meditation or praying practices or equivalent).

Choose your timeframe.

Close your eyes and listen.

Listen to your heartbeat.

Pay attention to how you breathe with closed eyes.

Write down your first thoughts on what came up.

Chapter 8: Tuning into Forgiveness and Making Amends

Learn the history of your parents and ancestors:

Ask the right questions.

Be patient.

Ask for permission to ask about sensitive information.

Be polite and kind.

Be respectful.

What to do with uncomfortable situations:

Don't run away from the uncomfortable situation. (Make sure to seek professional help when required.)

Address the uncomfortable situation.

Clear them up - Heal all wounds- Heal your emotions.

Questions you need to ask yourself:

Are you concerned about accomplishing things "at your age"?

Do you hear negative self-talk within yourself?

Is your self-talk telling you that you are too young or too old to accomplish something?

Can I forgive those who harmed me?

Do I need to stay in contact with them?

Remember:

Nobody is perfect.

Any past experiences are life lessons.

Any bad or negative feelings can be transmuted into positive feelings.

No negative situation is permanent.

Write down your thoughts.

Remember your stages of growing up:

Find out about the early stages of your life 1-10 years.

Find out about your life from 11-20 years.

Find out about your life from 21-35 years.

Look for familiar patterns.

Check if you need to change them or if they are part of your purpose.

Learn to Forgive:

Verbally - Written - Energetically - Learn to let go - Forgiving is not the same as forgetting.

Practice positive self-talk:

Observe your negative self-talk.

Replace it with positive self-talk.

Find out what you truly want.

Create a plan of what you need.

Action it with a positive approach.

Believe in yourself.

Recommended: Find someone who is going to help you to be accountable.

Recommended: Be accountable and responsible for your thinking and your actions.

Chapter 9: Creating a Pleasant Environment in Your Workplace, No Matter What

How can you adapt to suffering from migraines?

(Find the suitable registered professional to help you with each category.)

Choose to act.

Start to exercise.

Learn to meditate or follow your religious practice.

Train yourself to eat well.

Choose lighter and healthier foods.

Be consistent with your new habits and routines.

Begin to improve your brain capacity.

Allow yourself to learn more.

Continue to manage stress daily by doing the following:

Choose person-centred meditations or a religious practice or equivalent.

Practise appropriate exercises suitable for you.

Eat healthy, lighter food.

Focus on what your body needs rather than what you want.

What you can do if you do not like something at your workplace:

Find a way to improve the situation.

Do this without interfering with company policies and procedures.

Challenge yourself - Learn more about yourself.

Recommendation:

Prioritise five things to learn.

Master those before you move on to the next level.

Create a vision board for each part of your life with the five priorities in mind.

Use the question, "Why?"

Determine who you are.

Determine who you want to be.

Find out what you represent.

Focus on each priority daily.

Synchronise the priorities to complement each one of them daily.

By mastering your future:

You know what your purpose is.

You know what your idea for an invention is.

You know who it is for.

You remember to include like-minded people in your future and prioritise caring for planet earth as well.

When you master the principles of past, present, and future, your self-respect is reflected in like-minded people's minds.

You become connected.

You find the group of people who will follow you.

You find the right people who will help you to achieve/accomplish your purpose.

Chapter 10: Becoming a United Transcended Business Leader

Questions to ask:

Have you ever lost things?

Do you forget where you put your keys or your documents?

Where did you put it?

Which folder is it in?

The Importance of Organisational Skills in Business:

Recommended: (Seek the appropriate help from a registered professional.)

Prioritise time management.

Organise your paperwork.

Develop a system for organizing your files.

Ensure your environment is tidy.

Understand time management.

Prioritise tasks.

Set up your business plan.

Set up a strategic plan.

Have a plan to reach your goal.

Have a strategy in place.

Be organised and efficient.

Schedule your time wisely.

Exercise your mind and your memory.

Paperwork and Documentation:

Know where your folders are, to save time.

Remember GDPR and data protection requirements. (Seek appropriate professional help.)

Be efficient.

Make specific files.

Make sure you have sub-files, to eliminate confusion.

Have a folder of people in an industry you need to keep in touch with.

Each of them has a different purpose.

Have both filing systems, physical files on your desk, and electronic files on your computer.

Keep your files organised and consistent.

Budget.

Have team management (when required).

Marketing and sales:

(Seek appropriate professional help to protect your idea and yourself.)

Know the product or service.

Know the origin of the product.

Introduce your idea.

Give it some thought.

Introduce it to people who have a similar idea.

Be passionate about your idea.

Let others see how authentic you are with your project.

Make it happen.

Let people join you/your team.

"Persistent thinking and brainstorming can help you to develop business relationships and partnerships that could lead to an enormous empire of united transcended business leaders. These leaders could be just the change that will help Planet Earth become a better place."

—Marki Spacilova

The Legal Requirements:

Decide who to include in your team.

Be aware of standard business systems.

Have the right insurance.

Have a bookkeeping system in place.

Copyrighting or trademark.

Understand the legal requirements that you'll need to handle.

Market your business; what is the point of creating something only for yourself?

Some of the Requirements of a transcended business leader:

Willing to accept responsibility for your thinking and your actions.

Willing to obey all legal requirements.

Willing to have Commitment, Consistency, and the Courage to become the CEO of your life is a MUST.

Willing to make a difference for the people and planet Earth

Willing to let the world see your idea.

Willing to choose the materials you use.

Willing to choose the people you work with wisely.

Willing to choose to become a united transcended business leader.

Willing to collaborate, brainstorm, and build the community for united transcended business leaders.

Some of the requirements of a united transcended business leader:

Willing to think of the effectiveness of the materials you use, and the environment.

Willing to become eco-friendly and use sustainable materials in your business.

Willing to use a code of ethics.

Willing to use a code of conduct.

Willing to create and use a code of ethnicity, diversity, and inclusion.

Willing to create and use a code of gratitude, respect, and dignity.

Without collaboration with an appropriate registered trained professional, and choosing to do all the exercises by yourself, you are hereby taking the risks and you are taking responsibility for your thinking and your actions and results in your life.

Are You Ready to Step into Your next Level?

WHAT CAN YOU DO TO START?

1. Find out what do you truly want.
2. Increase your self-confidence and self-esteem with empowerment.
3. Break through your problems, obstacles, or challenges with ease to become wiser.
4. Get the support you need to lead you to the next level in your life.
5. Start here and step into your next level:

6. Join me with co-marketing partnership
7. Join me with affiliate programs
8. Receive bonus every time you take the next step to higher level in your life!

ACKNOWLEDGEMENT OF CREDIBILITY IN THEIR EXPERTISE

I want to say thank you to those who participated in interviews when I was doing my research regarding this book. Without those people, I would not have completed this book successfully such as Christopher Robertson - Intellectual property consultant, Michael Wilson - Fitness, Indy Bansil - Holistic Health Therapist, Karine Patel - Nutritionist/Dietician, Khyam Chudry - Accountancy, James Heath - Yoga, Michelle Gibbs – Art and Gallery, and many more.

Printed in Great Britain
by Amazon

11337496R00062